NEWCASTLE'S GRAINGER TOW

An Urban Renaissance

© English Heritage 2003

Text by Fiona Cullen (Newcastle City Council) and David Lovie (English Heritage)
Project coordinated by Colum Giles
New photographs by Bob Skingle and Tony Perry
Photographic printing by Bob Skingle
Maps by Tony Berry

Edited and brought to press by Adèle Campbell
Designed by Michael McMann
Printed by BAS Printers, Salisbury, Wiltshire

ISBN: 1 873592 77 9
Product code: 50811

English Heritage is the Government's statutory advisor on all aspects of the historic environment.
23 Savile Row, London W1S 2ET
Telephone 020 7973 3000
www.english-heritage.org.uk

The National Monuments Record is the public archive of English Heritage. All records and photography created while working on this project are available there. For more information contact NMR Enquiry and Research Service, National Monuments Record, Kemble Drive, Swindon SN2 2GZ. Telephone 01793 414600

The Grainger Town Partnership and Newcastle City Council made financial contributions towards the publication of this book.

NEWCASTLE'S GRAINGER TOWN
An Urban Renaissance

Text by Fiona Cullen and David Lovie

Photographs by Bob Skingle and Tony Perry

Maps by Tony Berry

Gilded clock on the corner of Blackett Street and Pilgrim Street. [DP000128]

Contents

Foreword

Conservation has transformed many run-down historic areas and we need to celebrate these successes. All concerned with the historic environment gain strength through the demonstration that it can play a vital role in the life of our towns and of our countryside, now and in the future. It is also important to show that conservation is not just about the details of buildings: it acts within a wider context that includes the economic and social well-being of places, and helps to define what these places should be. Conservation is far more than simply a matter of what buildings look like: it concerns the quality of our lives in the places where we work and play.

Grainger Town is one such success story. It fulfils a number of aspirations for the historic environment. In the life of the partnership that led its regeneration, it was transformed from a city-centre area with serious doubts over its future into a quarter with a new sense of purpose and a new self-confidence. The magnificent architectural heritage and the unique assemblages of spaces which make up Grainger Town have received the attention and care they deserve, but these improvements are underpinned and sustained by a transformation in the way in which the area is used. The Grainger Town Project has injected new economic life into the quarter and demonstrated new ways in which we can use and enjoy our city centres. The key has been to bring people back to the area once again, and with people come economic and social gain. The process has worked. Grainger Town is thronging by day and full of activity at night, and all this set against an architectural backdrop of unrivalled quality and interest. But what is most heartening is to sense the pride with which the people of Newcastle regard their city. Instead of a depressing quarter with an uncertain future, they now have a centre second to none among great European cities.

The story of Grainger Town old and new is well worth the telling, for it has lessons for us all in how historic places can exploit their unique character in the modern world. But the key test of a project's achievements is sustainable success. There is every expectation that the Grainger Town Project has created the conditions for this to happen. It has already exceeded all our expectations. For now, we can enjoy the project's achievement and in the future we will work together, with others, to guarantee continuing good health.

Sir Neil Cossons
Chairman, English Heritage

Councillor Tony Flynn
Leader, Newcastle City Council
and Chairman, Grainger Town Partnership

(facing page) Grey Street, Theatre Royal [AA040882]

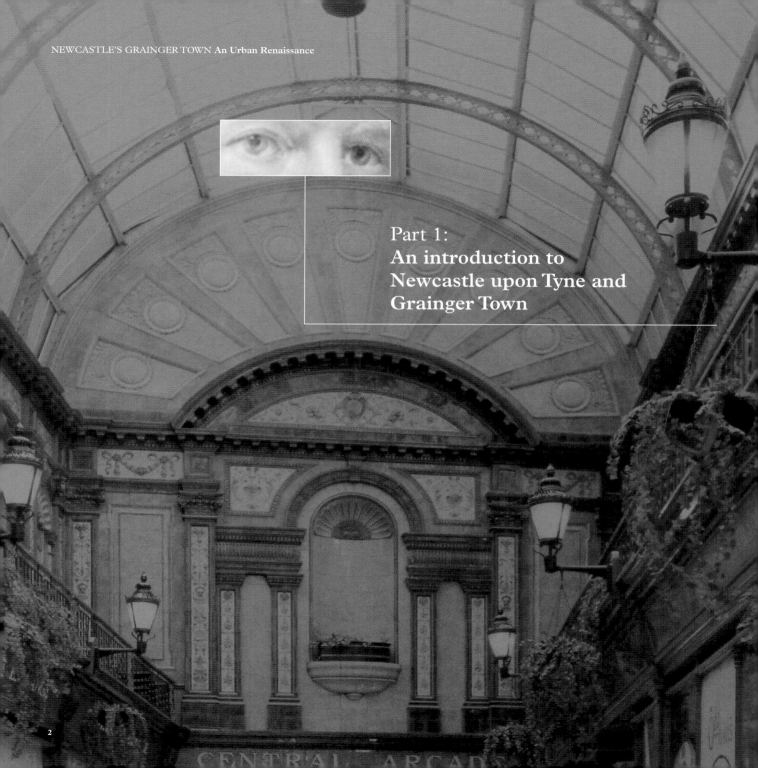

Part 1:
An introduction to Newcastle upon Tyne and Grainger Town

Two things which the eye can see and the aesthetic sense appreciate distinguish Newcastle from Leeds or Bradford or Sheffield or any other industrial city of the North. One is the river, the other Richard Grainger ... In what way Grainger's work forms a special distinction needs nowadays hardly be emphasized. He gave the whole centre of the town a dignity and orderliness which even the twentieth century has not succeeded in destroying.

Grundy *et al* 1992, 408

Introduction

Grainger Town is as much an idea as it is a place. It is not a concept that is familiar to people from outside Newcastle and its hinterland, but it is an important phenomenon, both historically and in today's debate about conservation in our cities and towns. The name identifies the prime mover behind one of the most significant exercises in urban planning in the middle decades of the 19th century. Richard Grainger, a native of Newcastle and a builder and speculator unparalleled in the region, was the coordinator of a radical replanning that turned the town of his birth from an already handsome regional capital to one which excited the admiration of visitors from far and wide. Grainger's particular achievement was to create a new commercial and residential heart within a historic town, a heart with a consistent architectural quality starkly different from the piecemeal and eclectic character of most northern industrial cities. His style was classical, and his work and the region's taste for Grecian architecture have together made the term 'Tyneside Classical' an accepted descriptive label.

Grainger's contribution to Newcastle was acknowledged even as his scheme was in the process of building, and his reputation became so great that his name has never been forgotten in the town. Few builders and speculators in other towns have enjoyed such prolonged recognition. Over time, what Grainger achieved in Newcastle came to overshadow many other significant elements of the town's character, and it is only a slight exaggeration to suggest that, for the architectural historian, mention of Newcastle brings Grainger's name first to mind. When, in the early 1990s, a project was initiated to regenerate a substantial part of the historic core of Newcastle, including all of Grainger's work of the 1830s, it was natural to apply the name of the dominating spirit of the place to the project and by extension to the area it embraced. So 'Grainger Town' was born: a name with the potential to confuse, but one solidly based on the history of the place.

The Grainger Town which is the subject of this book does, however, extend beyond the streets developed by Richard Grainger. It includes a substantial part of the historic core of the town, including the medieval market place and much of the area that lay within the medieval town walls. The boundaries of the planning zone were drawn not with uniform historic character in mind, but instead to include those quarters of the city that were most in need of a rapid programme of regeneration. As a result, Grainger Town is a fascinating mix, and its study has served to highlight the significant survival, in the modern city, of much of the grain of the medieval town, of ancient plot boundaries and open spaces, and of important evidence of urban development dating from long before Grainger got to work. The character of Grainger Town is one of diversity and contrast: different ages of building, different scales, different activities in different quarters. For the most part, the quality is good and rises in places to the superlative. This book describes the evolution of the area and explains how recent planning initiatives, coordinated by the Grainger Town Partnership, have celebrated and exploited a unique urban landscape and injected new life into it.

Historic Newcastle

Because Newcastle has, in the popular imagination, the image of an industrial city like Manchester or Leeds, many people assume that it does not have a long history; industrial cities are not expected to be old. But even a short acquaintance with Newcastle's townscape and history reveals that the city first flourished under the Romans, when it was known as Pons Aelius, and that it received its present name under the Normans.

Location is the key to Newcastle's long history. It was the reason for its foundation and continued to be of vital significance in later periods. The town is situated at the end of one of the two east–west passes through the northern Pennines, it lies on the main north–south route down the eastern side of England, and (as it still does today) it provided the lowest bridging point over the Tyne, itself a route to the outside world. Lying ten miles inland, the town was also less exposed in the past to raiders and pirates than settlements on the coast.

The Roman name for the town gives two clues to its early history. The settlement first developed around the strategically important bridge, the *pons*, built by the Romans (Fig 1). It was integrated into the defensive system that we know today as Hadrian's Wall: the Emperor's family name was Aelius. The wall, visible above ground in places in the western suburbs, has been obscured in the modern town centre, but emerges to the east to terminate at Wallsend Fort (Segedunum). A fort was built on the hill above the bridge in the late 2nd century AD to bolster the defences, and a civilian settlement, a *vicus*, developed around the fort, supporting and doubtless profiting from it. Pons Aelius did not enjoy the same high status as Corstopitum (Corbridge) to the west which, being on Dere Street, the principal Roman north–south route, was a substantial arsenal and supply base, but nevertheless it had an important role in protecting the easternmost flank of the wall and defending the bridge over the Tyne. The outline of part of the fort and its buildings has been laid out following excavations in the Castle Garth area.

Under the stress of invasion the Roman Empire began to break up. Early in the 5th century AD the Romans withdrew from the province of Britain and Pons Aelius began to crumble. For the next two centuries Britain was colonised by settlers from the European mainland, and in the north-east there developed the powerful Anglian kingdom of Northumbria.

Fig 1 *The swing bridge of 1868–76, which replaced an earlier stone arched bridge, swings on a central axis to allow ships to pass. The keep of the castle, on the site of the Roman fort, overlooks the river crossing. [DP000124]*

Under rulers like King Edwin a Christian culture of national importance flourished, led by gifted men like Bendict Biscop and Bede, a monk at nearby Jarrow and possibly the greatest of all Anglo-Saxon scholars. Whether a settlement on the site of Newcastle played a part in Northumbria's golden age is not clear: all we know is that a village or town called Monkchester occupied the north bank of the Tyne in this period.

The establishment of a Norman kingdom after 1066 brought disaster to large parts of the north of England. Native resistance led to savage repression and large tracts were laid waste on the orders of King William, in ruthless reprisal for acts of defiance like the murder of the Norman Bishop of Durham and Northumberland in Gateshead on 14 May 1080. The Normans quickly grasped the strategic significance of the site of Newcastle and the importance of integrating it into a network of defensive strongholds. Robert Curthose, William's eldest son, built the first castle on the site of the Roman fort, overlooking the rebuilt Roman bridge. It had an earth mound topped by a wooden tower and surrounded by a fortified bailey, and was probably the structure that gave the town the name by which it has been known ever since. The wooden tower was replaced under Henry II by a much grander stone keep and castle, built between 1168 and 1178 (Fig 2).

The chronic disputes and violence between the kingdoms of England and Scotland in the Middle Ages threatened stability and hindered urban development. Newcastle attempted to provide security by the construction of a defensive town wall, begun in the late 13th century. The wall was to prove its worth on several occasions, but finally lost its military purpose in the years of stability that followed the suppression of the Jacobite rising of 1745. Much was destroyed in the 18th and 19th centuries, but the surviving fabric represents one of the best surviving medieval town walls in England.

The construction of the wall had a profound effect on the town, providing the security necessary for the flourishing of its domestic, commercial and religious life. By the middle of the 15th century Newcastle, with a population of 4,000, contained the precincts of at least eight religious houses, more than a dozen hospitals, four parish

Fig 2 Henry II's great keep towers over the railway line and was once the central part of the royal castle. [AA040913]

churches of Norman foundation, a merchants' quarter by the river and extensive markets of all kinds on the higher ground. The wealth of the town was derived from the export of hides and wool, increasingly supplemented by the rapidly developing export of coal. The coal industry was already well established around Newcastle by the 13th century and grew progressively over the following centuries to bring great prosperity to the town and its region.

Something of the medieval town's size and character can be seen in John Speed's plan of Newcastle, published in 1610 (Fig 3). More of a diagram than a measured map, it shows the complete circuit of the town wall and the developing suburbs outside the wall at Westgate, Barras Bridge and Gallowgate. The castle appears as an insignificant enclosure, giving little indication of its original importance. A single bridge across the Tyne, nine religious establishments and a higher density of buildings and people along the crowded riverside are illustrated. The map marks two features that will be of great relevance later in the story of Grainger Town: the stream – the Lort Burn – that runs north–south dividing the town in two; and the 'Newe House', in its own extensive grounds between Bigg Market and Pilgrim Street. Only with the removal of both these barriers – one physical, the other resulting from land ownership – could the town be remodelled to Grainger's great plan.

The story of Newcastle in the 17th and 18th centuries is one of growing trade, especially in coal, greater density of building as the town wall began to constrict growth and the development of an increasingly sophisticated local elite. A new age of elegance is reflected in a number of architectural features in the town. New houses were now built in brick or stone rather than timber: the best early brick house is Alderman Fenwick's residence on Pilgrim Street, and good examples of 18th-century houses survive on Westgate. The town's great showpieces, introducing new ideas of planning and design, include Charlotte Square (1770) and the Assembly Rooms in Westgate Road (1775), both by local architect William Newton (Fig 4).

Fig 3 *Speed's map of 1610 shows the compact nature of the medieval city.*

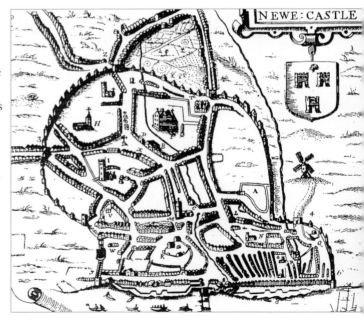

In this prosperous town the inconvenience represented by the Lort Burn began to be a serious obstacle to urban life, impeding east–west movement across the town as well as movement up from the Quayside. In 1774 the Newcastle Corporation, which controlled many of the town's activities, decided to culvert a section of the Burn to enable a new street – Dean Street – to connect the Quayside and the upper part

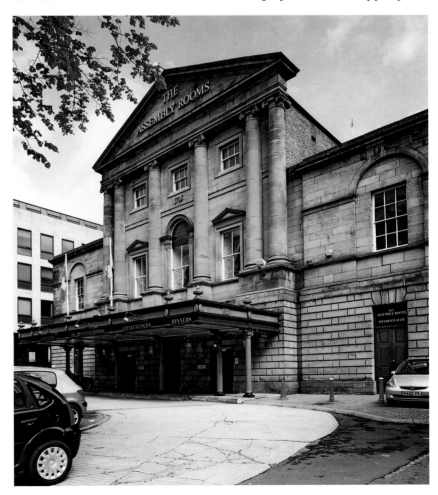

Fig 4 *The Assembly Rooms, Fenkle Street, built 1774–6 to designs by local architect William Newton.* [AA040530]

of the town, and the new Mosley and Collingwood Streets to be pushed through between Pilgrim Street and Westgate Street. The works also created a new site for the Flesh Market, relocated from near Bigg Market. These town improvements made access easier around the growing centre and provided more space and better sanitary conditions for the expanded Flesh Market needed to feed the growing population of the town, which in 1800 had reached 28,000.

These planned changes were an opportunity to introduce a new dignity and uniformity to the townscape. The local architect David Stephenson (1756–1819) was given the task of devising design guidelines for the Corporation's new streets. He stipulated that buildings should be a standard three storeys in height and of brick with stone dressings, a style which provided an elegant precursor to Richard Grainger's grand designs. Ironically, Stephenson's streets became such a commercial success throughout the 19th and early 20th centuries that they were extensively redeveloped and only a handful of his buildings survive to hint at the former quality of the area.

The barrier to outward expansion represented by the town wall was progressively removed from the middle of the 18th century. By 1770 all the wall along the quay had been demolished, and Thomas Oliver's map of 1830 shows that other long stretches to the north and east had been removed, enabling the town to begin to expand outwards in virtually all directions (Fig 5). Oliver's map is especially interesting as it introduces Richard Grainger to the story, for it shows most of the building work that he undertook before he embarked on his new town centre for Newcastle. Included are houses in Higham Place (1819); terraces in Blackett Street (begun in 1824); the fine houses of Eldon Square (begun in 1825); more terraces in St Mary's Place (1827); and the splendid terraces of Leazes Terrace, Crescent and Place (1829). In 1834 Richard Grainger, then aged 37, published his master plan for the town and began the political and economic processes that were to transform Newcastle from a handsome regional centre to one of national distinction in its planning and design.

Fig 5 *The medieval street pattern is still evident on Oliver's map of 1830, which also shows how crowded the area within the walls had become.*

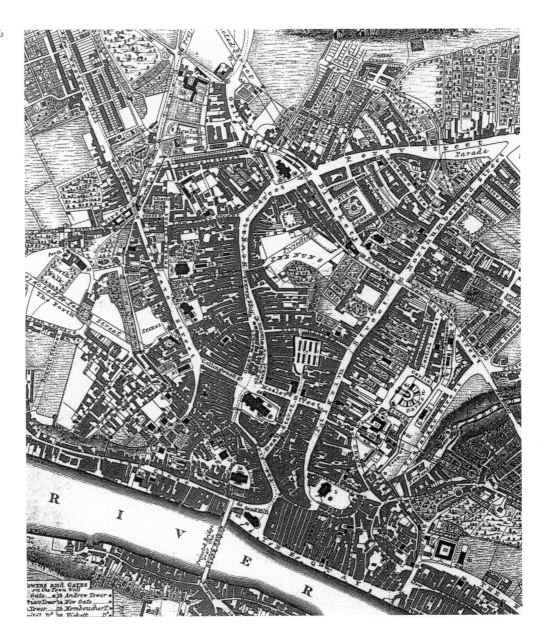

Richard Grainger

Richard, the youngest of four sons of Thomas and Amelia Grainger, was born on 9 October 1797. The family occupied rooms in a poor tenement in High Friar Lane, just inside the crumbling town wall on the line of what is now Blackett Street. This run-down quarter of Newcastle was close to the extensive enclosing walls of Anderson Place, previously known as 'Newe House' and named thus on Speed's plan of 1610. Within 25 years Richard himself would begin to clear this whole area of town wall, tenements and big houses to make way for his grand scheme.

Richard's father was a labourer from Cumberland while his mother, born in Gibraltar in 1755, was the daughter of a serving soldier. She was particularly resourceful and after the early death of her husband her skills at sewing, glove-making and laundering linen continued to support her five children – a daughter, also named Amelia, was born in 1794.

Richard's education at St Andrew's Parish Charity School in Percy Street was rudimentary. By the time he left school his elder brother, George, was already apprenticed to a bricklayer, and Richard followed him into the building trade. In 1809 he was indentured to John Brown, a house carpenter and builder, and in 1816 George and Richard began in business together as jobbing builders. They started in a small way, their first significant job reputed to be the reconstruction of a neighbour's house in High Friar Lane. George's untimely death in 1817 left Richard to carry on the business alone; numbers 3–6 Strawberry Place are the first houses that Richard built on his own.

In 1819, possibly through his connections with Methodism, Richard first met the man who was to set him on the road to success. Alderman William Batson commissioned the young Grainger to construct a number of middle-class houses in Higham Place, a new street outside the town walls. This was an up-and-coming residential quarter and Richard went on to build further houses in the area: in Percy Street, New Bridge Street and Carliol Street. Some of his Higham Place houses still survive but the others from this early period of his work have gone (Fig 6).

Fig 6 *Higham Place, built by Richard Grainger in 1819. [AA040543]*

Two years later, in 1821, Richard married Rachel Arundale, daughter of a wealthy and prominent businessman in the leather trade. The enhanced social status and, more particularly, the substantial dowry that Richard received from this advantageous marriage enabled him to extend his business. In 1824 he built 31 houses, to designs by architect Thomas Oliver, in Blackett Street, a new street created by the demolition the previous year of the crumbling stretch of town wall close to Richard's birthplace. With this job Richard acquired the status of a substantial builder in the town, and from then on there was no stopping him.

A major development, in both the townscape of Newcastle and the reputation of Richard Grainger, came in 1825 with the building of Eldon Square, again to designs by Oliver, later modified by architect John Dobson. The square was designed very much on the London model, with houses on three sides of a communal garden (Fig 7). The square, with its fine ashlar masonry and elegant classical detailing, was not completed until 1832 when the Northern Counties Club finally opened, in the central section of the northern terrace. Dobson also designed Grainger's St Mary's Place (1827) (Fig 8), adding a gentle Gothic flavour to complement the nearby St Thomas's Church. Thomas Oliver was responsible for the magnificent design of Leazes Terrace, which Grainger began in 1829 (Fig 9), and the final offering of this winning spell of grand Georgian buildings was the Royal Arcade in Pilgrim Street, designed by Dobson and completed in 1832.

In July 1833 the Mayor of Newcastle held a great public dinner to mark the town's appreciation of Richard Grainger's extraordinary contribution to its streets and public life. Grainger, then aged 36, was presented with a silver tureen and salver. Although Grainger did not introduce Georgian splendour into Newcastle – this had been done by architects such as David Stephenson and William Newton in the late 18th century – he was responsible for its full flowering, and by 1833 his total output was valued at £195,000. Grainger's greatest achievement, however, was yet to come. Hitherto he had worked within the grain of the existing town, modifying and improving it. But now he entered on a wholly different scale of operation, one that resulted in a dramatic

Fig 7 *Eldon Square. Built 1825–32, the square had houses on three sides, but much was lost when the modern shopping centre was built. [AA040545]*

Fig 8 *St Mary's Place. Dobson's design of 1827 was an unusual exercise in Tudor Gothic. [AA040542]*

Fig 9 *Leazes Terrace. This residential development, designed by Thomas Oliver and built by Grainger, was a huge project; evidence of Grainger's growing ability to undertake large contracts. [AA040541]*

remodelling of large parts of the town and a new identity for this northern capital. The new centre that he built between 1834 and 1842 singles Newcastle out as uniquely beautiful amongst those English cities that grew as industry and commerce developed in the 19th century.

As Grainger enters the limelight it is interesting to assess what sort of man he was (Fig 10). As a child he had a quiet manner, but as he

Fig 10 *Richard Grainger in later life, portrait by David Mossman. Grey Street and the Theatre Royal are recognisable in the background. [Reproduced by kind permission of the Laing Art Gallery, Newcastle]*

grew older this proved to be a sign not of diffidence but of confidence and hard-headedness, characteristics often remarked upon throughout his life. Like many entrepreneurs of the period Grainger was essentially a man of business, ruthless when necessary in pushing through his vision. He was not particularly philanthropic – he never built for the lower classes – but he improved everyone's life, risking bankruptcy in the process, by providing a graceful urban environment with handsome streets and a stock of fine, durable buildings far more elaborate and grand than they needed to be. He was known as a private man not given to socialising and unlike many of his aspiring contemporaries he kept himself out of the political arena. In his lifetime he was lionised by the town but his financial difficulties, culminating in 1839 in his inability to pay his creditors, soured some against him.

Of course Grainger's achievement was not the result of his own unaided effort. The late 18th and early 19th centuries saw the flourishing of a talented group of architects in the Newcastle area: William Newton's work at the Assembly Rooms and Charlotte Square has been mentioned, as has Stephenson's work in Dean Street. Other architects who made major contributions to the region before Grainger's day include Sir Charles Monck, who built Belsay Hall as an early exercise in Greek Revival in 1807, and John Stokoe, who designed the Moot Hall (1810–12), the first Greek Revival building in Newcastle. Grainger was fortunate in being able to call on the services of the next generation of architects, some with an established reputation in the area. Grainger worked closely with Thomas Oliver, John Dobson, and John and Benjamin Green, and he also employed his own able local architects George Walker and John Wardle. His social progress, which allowed him to secure wealthy clients, was assisted by his marriage and by men such as Alderman Batson and John Fenwick, who acted as his attorney. But above all Grainger was indebted to John Clayton, town clerk of Newcastle and, from 1834 until Grainger's death in 1861, his personal solicitor and private advisor. More than once Clayton's wise counsel and insistence on early action saved him from bankruptcy. It was Clayton who persuaded Grainger to return to face the music in 1841 after he had fled the town in panic to escape his creditors.

Grainger received the most steadfast support from his wife. Rachel Grainger conducted his correspondence and kept his accounts until his business activities became too complicated. She then concentrated on bringing up their family, which finally totalled thirteen children (six sons and seven daughters), all but two of whom reached maturity. She died in childbirth in Scotland, in 1842, one of Grainger's darkest years. Grainger soon took up residence in one of his own terraces at No. 36 Clayton Street West (Fig 11a) and used offices a few doors away at number No. 28 (Fig 11b). On 14 July 1861, after instructing his men and while attending to the rest of the day's work, he was suddenly taken ill and within half an hour died of what was diagnosed as heart disease. The town was plunged into mourning, the minute bell of St Nicholas's Church was tolled, and shopkeepers in Grainger's streets boarded up their premises as a mark of respect. Although Grainger had worked hard to clear his debts, at his death he still owed £128,000 while his personal estate amounted to only £17,000. But Clayton's skills and rising land values allowed the last of the debts to be cleared by 1901, by which time Grainger's estate was valued at £1,202,087.

Figs 11a & b Commemorative plaques in Clayton Street West at Grainger's former residence (above left) [DP00089] and offices (above). [DP00088]

Grainger's Newcastle

Grainger's great scheme of urban redevelopment involved nothing less than the relandscaping of a substantial part of the built-up area of Newcastle. The key to the scheme was the 'Newe House' of Speed's map of 1610. In the Middle Ages the Benedictine nunnery of St Bartholomew had occupied a 12-acre site in the northern quarter of the town. After the dissolution of the monasteries in 1539, the land and buildings were acquired by a merchant, Robert Anderson, who built a fine mansion – Speed's 'Newe House' – within the site. The house was later acquired by the Blackett family and then by a wealthy builder, by coincidence also named Anderson. The property, then Anderson Place, was again for sale in 1826, and the availability of this excellent piece of real estate, an undeveloped hole in the centre of Newcastle, was to serve as the spring-board for Richard Grainger's great scheme.

Both John Dobson and Thomas Oliver had produced plans for the redevelopment of Anderson Place in the late 1820s but it was Grainger's plan, more commercial in its emphasis than those of his rivals, that was set before the Newcastle Common Council on 22 May 1834 with, of course, the support of the town clerk John Clayton. To help people understand the plan Thomas Sopwith, local historian and surveyor, was commissioned to produce an isometric view of the scheme for public display, copies of which survive, dated 11 June 1834. Grainger proposed to acquire land south and north of Anderson Place to create a continuous block of land linking the recently created streets of the southern town (Mosley and Collingwood Streets) with the newly completed elegance of Eldon Square and Blackett Street, that Grainger had helped to create outside the old walls to the north. The area for development was increased by the completion of the culverting of the Lort Burn, for so long a barrier within the town.

Within this area Grainger planned two main streets, Grey Street and Grainger Street, converging on a circus which, with a new Gothic-style town hall and existing nearby churches, was to become a new civic focus for the town (Fig 12). A third main route, Clayton Street, occupied the western part of the plan. Short straight roads were to link

Fig 12 *View of Grey Street (left) and Grainger Street (right) from the top of Grey's Monument, with the Central Exchange Buildings in the foreground. [DP000130]*

the new streets with each other and with Bigg Market and Pilgrim Street, forming a network of wide thoroughfares and grand architecture. In his street layout Grainger rejected a simple grid plan, and instead based his scheme on three triangles; it is difficult to find English precedents for this arrangement. In addition to the town hall Grainger also proposed replacements for the Flesh Market (1808) and the old Theatre Royal (1788, by David Stephenson), both of which would be swept away by the plan. Within this overall layout the streets were to be lined with palace-fronted terraces in a classical style. Further variety and interest were introduced to the terraces by the use of end and central pavilions sporting tall columns (Fig 13). This style has since become known locally as 'Tyneside Classical'.

Hitherto dominated by complex patterns of land ownership and by the resulting individualistic and piecemeal character of street frontages, Newcastle now had at its very heart a designed landscape in which the parts were subordinated to the whole. Other towns had such quarters:

Fig 13 *52–78 Grey Street. The use of pavilions to break up the terrace elevations helps to accommodate the fall of the land to the south. [AA040921]*

Fig 14 *Grainger Street. The frontage to Grainger Market, made up of three-bay units designed to give a shop on the ground floor and living accommodation over. One of the 14 entrances to the market can be seen in this view. [AA040918]*

18th-century London, Bath and Edinburgh had their squares and terraces, and parts of inner Liverpool are still dominated by long rows of uniform early 19th-century housing. But where Grainger's work stands out is in the nature of the development, which was at the same time both residential and commercial. In his earlier work on the margins of the town Grainger had built houses for the well-to-do, but his new site was right in the town centre and success lay in exploiting this to provide not just a genteel area for living but also a thriving business district: a reminder that the two were not seen as mutually exclusive in the 19th century. Banks, a market, an exchange and offices were incorporated into the plans, along with cultural facilities, but numerically the dominant building type was the combined shop and house, 325 of which were planned. For much of the length of Grainger's principal streets a standard three-bay unit provided a shop on the ground floor and two or three storeys of housing above (Fig 14). Contemporary schemes on the European mainland would have provided apartments but the English preferred houses, so that is what

Grainger built: some very grand ones in Grey Street and smaller ones for artisans and trades people in Clayton Street. Perhaps the closest comparison with Grainger's work, in scale and conception, is John Nash's Regent Street in London, which in part at least displayed the same combination of domestic and business accommodation within a grand scheme. But while Nash's work has largely perished, Grainger's survives.

Once Grainger received final approval from the Corporation on 12 June 1834 he moved with characteristic energy and drive. He concluded the purchase of Anderson Place and within two weeks work had begun on site. The rate of progress and scale of operation were to amaze the townspeople for the next few years. Huge amounts of soil and other materials were moved around to re-contour the area and Grainger set up a brickworks on the site to make use of the clay his men were turning up. Astonishingly, by 4 October the foundations of the replacement market were in place, one range of shops was completed and so were the foundations for Grainger Street. He signed an agreement to replace the old Theatre Royal and, to the regret of many, he began the demolition of Stephenson's handsome little theatre within three hours of purchase. Both replacement market and theatre each took Grainger less than twelve months to complete.

Such a flurry of activity had its problems. The whole town was severely disrupted: stone and timber delivery carts clogged the streets, dust, mud and dirt were everywhere and many streets were often blocked by scaffolding. Only one building accident is recorded, when the collapse of three partly built houses on Market Street killed seven men and injured at least eight others, some severely. Minutes before, Grainger had been inspecting this work and at the time of the collapse was on scaffolding around an adjoining building. A lightning strike was finally deemed to have been responsible for the accident.

Grainger's houses were built according to traditional principles with much of their strength being in the outer and inner skins of stone in the decorative façade. Rear walls were of brick, and timber floors tied the structure together. Although this reflected standard building practice, the buildings had faults that time would reveal. The brick and rubble party walls were not tied in with the front and back walls and a few properties have since required stitching together. In others, timbers inserted into the inside of the façades for levelling off the masonry have been responsible for outbreaks of dry rot, often exacerbated by inadequate maintenance of external and internal drainpipes.

By about 1842 most of the three main streets and the six interconnecting streets were complete and occupied, although some upper floors had been put to uses other than housing, such as warehousing and an incorporated company's hall. Over the years, much of the residential space would give way to offices, restaurants and cafés as Grainger's centre became more and more commercial in nature.

Most of Grainger's new streets have retained their original names. Grainger Street and Clayton Street were named after the prime movers behind the scheme, and Nelson Street was named after the national hero. Nun Street commemorates the old nunnery of St Bartholomew while Hood Street was called after John Lionel Hood, Mayor of Newcastle in 1834–5; no doubt a wise political choice at the time. Our national bard is recognised by Shakespeare Street which appropriately runs along the south side of Grainger's new Theatre Royal. The only street to change its name is the principal thoroughfare from Mosley Street to Blackett Street. Originally intended to be named Upper or New Dean Street, it became Grey Street once it was decided that a massive monument to Earl Grey (whose name was given to a type of tea) should be built at the pivotal point of the great scheme to commemorate his contribution to the passing of the Great Reform Bill in 1832.

Grainger's achievement

Richard Grainger's astonishing achievement in such a short time received immediate acclaim. In 1840 Harriet Martineau, the pioneering female journalist, described how nearly a million pounds had been added to the value of the town by Grainger's work in just five years.

The new developments included ten inns, twelve public houses, forty private houses and 325 houses with shops as well as nine new streets and many individual public buildings such as the market, central exchange, the theatre, a dispensary, a music hall and two chapels. Grainger was also ahead of his time in providing water closets, a provision noted by the Cholera Inquiry Commissioners in 1854.

Grainger's contribution to Newcastle has been recognised in a number of official commemorations. A major street and the huge indoor market that he built were given his name; in 1882 his daughter, Rachel Elizabeth Burns, arranged for a small public fountain to be erected in Neville Street (now standing in Waterloo Street) (Fig 15a); and in 1888 a Gothic memorial was placed on an inside wall of Grainger's parish church, St John's, appropriately in Grainger Street (*see* Fig 44b). There was then a lull of over a century until 1997, when Newcastle City Council and the Grainger Town Partnership commemorated Grainger's bicentenary with the erection of two circular commemorative plaques on his house and office in Clayton Street West (*see* Figs 11a and b).

Fig 15a *(above left) Grainger's commemorative fountain, now in Waterloo Street. [DP00092]*

Fig 15b *(above) Commemorative plate in Grainger Street. [DP00096]*

They also laid a huge metal plate in the pavement of the pedestrianised area at the top of Grainger Street. The artist who was commissioned to design this plate included some words that Richard Grainger might have used to address the people of his home town today: 'The past is my present to your future' (Fig 15b).

Grainger's work in Newcastle is on a large scale, but on a national level it is surpassed by that of other entrepreneurs. As a speculator and developer Thomas Cubitt, operating mainly in London, was responsible for a far larger quantity of building, although his work is more fragmented than Grainger's. Whole new towns were planned: Decimus Burton designed a new port at Fleetwood (although little was built); Ralph Jackson developed West Hartlepool as an east-coast port; and railway companies and entrepreneurs planned new towns as company headquarters and developed existing towns as leisure resorts.

The scale of these undertakings may have been greater than Grainger's in Newcastle, but Grainger's task was different: he operated within a crowded historic town to give it a new centre, an opportunity almost unprecedented until 20th-century planners got to work. He altered forever the way the town functioned and through the use of a monumental style created a new identity appropriate to Newcastle's role as a regional capital. However, long-term success for the new centre did not materialise: as soon as it was completed its character began to change and later developments in Newcastle created a new balance, leaving Grainger's work slightly marooned. But this partial failure cannot be blamed on Grainger, and it has had the beneficial effect of preserving for us today much of the original scheme. For the stranger to Newcastle today, the effect of Grainger's work is still startling and it is easy to appreciate why his contemporaries were so forcibly struck by his achievement. William Howitt's words, written in 1842, are as meaningful today as when he wrote them: 'You walk into what has long been termed the coal hole of the north and find yourself at once in a city of palaces; a fairyland of newness, brightness and modern elegance. And who has wrought this change? It is Mr. Grainger' (Howitt 1842, 310). A city of palaces indeed and, amazingly, virtually all of it survives to this day (Fig 16).

Fig 16 *33–9 Grey Street, the centrepiece of the west side of the street. [AA040886]*

The streets and buildings of Grainger Town

The part of central Newcastle that has been known as Grainger Town since 1991 includes much more than just Richard Grainger's Newcastle. In fact, Grainger's contribution covers only about a quarter of the area that was officially designated as 'Grainger Town' for the purposes of the six-year regeneration programme that terminated on 31 March 2003.

In addition to Grainger's marvellous classical legacy, Grainger Town includes areas and buildings of medieval origin such as Bigg and Cloth Markets, Blackfriars Dominican friary and a substantial section of Newcastle's town wall. Also included is Westgate, an old quarter inside the medieval walled town that contains some fine 18th- and 19th-century buildings. The historic Quayside, with its range of early houses and warehouses and later commercial buildings, and Dobson's great railway station on the plateau above the Tyne Gorge, lie outside the boundary of the regeneration area; otherwise, modern Grainger Town includes the bulk of the pre-1850 city and provides Newcastle with a historic heart of extraordinary richness and period quality.

Grainger Town naturally divides itself into four areas, each with a distinctive atmosphere derived, in the main, from its layout, architecture and use over the years. Hence this brief introduction to its streets and buildings is presented in four sections; more detail about many individual buildings is provided in the walking tour.

The old markets (8–13 in walking tour)

We do not know who laid out the triangular market area known as Bigg, Groat and Cloth Markets, but its simple geometric shape with narrow plots leading off indicates that it was a planned space and history suggests that it was likely to have been laid out in Norman times (Fig 17). The market places, burgage plots and narrow lanes serve as a reminder of the nature of the medieval town and contrast strongly with the regularity of Grainger's work.

All medieval English towns had their specialised markets and Newcastle is no exception. As well as the mixed cereal markets of Bigg and Groat, the area next to the cathedral was the Iron Market.

Fig 17 *Bigg Market at night. The width of the street shows its origin as a market place.* [AA040885]

The Cloth Market was converted at one point to become the town's Flesh Market, but reverted after 1808 to its earlier name. Both Groat and Cloth Market lanes were created by encroachments into the main market space, possibly from the late medieval period onwards. Vestiges of the early street markets still remain but the market area is now dominated by places to eat and drink, making it much busier at night than during the day.

Important buildings in the old market area include what was Newcastle's principal parish church, St Nicholas's, raised to cathedral status in 1882, with its outstanding 14th-century crown spire; architect Benjamin Simpson's jolly Half Moon public house, which in 1902 replaced a much earlier pub of the same name; the splendid Allied Irish Bank (formerly Lloyds) of 1890 in Collingwood Street; the attractively converted former Central Post Office of 1871; and the busy east side of Cloth Market which contains buildings (and fragments) of many early periods and styles, painted in many colours (Fig 18).

The Blackfriars precinct and town walls (32–36 in walking tour)

This north-west corner of the old walled town was dominated in the past by the Blackfriars precinct and St Andrew's Church, reputed to be the oldest of Newcastle's four medieval churches. After its suppression in 1539 the whole of the friary was acquired by the Corporation, which went on to lease the old cloister buildings to nine of the town's trade guilds, leaving the rest of the precinct as open ground for many years (Fig 19). Radical change to the quarter accelerated from the late 18th century. In 1770, the architect William Newton built Charlotte Square, Newcastle's earliest London-style square, on a corner of this open ground. The area around St Andrew's continued to be developed: the precinct was altered forever in the early 19th century when Stowell Street was driven through it and the rest was progressively encroached upon in a random way. Despite these changes the rear lane, ditch and town wall are still very much in evidence.

The area continued to develop in the late 19th and 20th centuries. Oliver and Leeson's 1898 row of Gallowgate shops and offices is presented in a delightful Free Baroque style. With its rich frontage and

Fig 18 *Cloth Market. The former market place is lined with a variety of buildings of many dates. [DP000125]*

Fig 19 *Blackfriars. The medieval friary was used after the dissolution by Newcastle's craft guilds as a meeting place and to provide almshouses. [AA040520]*

green copper onion dome it confidently turns the Gallowgate corner and the interest is continued at the back of the row, which is built directly on top of the town walls. Prominent later buildings include the vigorous conversion of Stowell Street into Newcastle's Chinatown from the early 1960s onwards (Fig 20), L G Ekins' excellent North East Co-operative store of 1931, and the bold treatment of the 1930s Magnet House and Andrews House in Gallowgate.

Grainger's streetscapes (1–7, 21–22 and 37–39 in the walking tour)
Much has already been made of Grainger's work in the last section. The 1830s composition of streets converging on the huge eye-catcher of Grey's Monument (Fig 21) is somewhat unusual in this country but the stopped-view theme is carried on throughout the plan. The western view along Shakespeare Street is stopped by a handsome pavilion on Grey Street and the views in both directions along Nelson and Nun Streets are terminated by sizeable pavilions or individually designed public houses: all part of Richard Grainger's planning and design genius.

Fig 20 *Colourful signage in Stowell Street, the centre of Newcastle's Chinese community. [DP00093]*

In the setting of Grainger's handsome palace-fronted terraces several buildings are outstanding. They include Grey's Monument (1838); Theatre Royal (1837); Central Exchange Building (1837); Lloyds Bank, Grey Street (1839); a former branch of the Bank of England (1835); and Grainger Market (1835). What is special about Grainger's streets is that the street layout and the grand buildings that line the frontages were part of the same overall plan, and this gives the landscape of this part of Grainger Town a unity and quality rarely found in major cities.

Westgate Road area and the Central Station (14–20 and 23–31 in the walking tour)

Westgate Road, the main route into the city from the west, is the only great medieval radial road of Newcastle that has not been diverted by new road building in the late 20th century. It still runs, as it always has, directly into the heart of the city.

Grainger took his Clayton Street across Westgate Road in the late 1830s, creating Clayton Street West on the south side, and did not

Fig 21 *(facing page) Grey's Monument provides a dramatic focus at the end of Grainger Street. [AA040887]*

hesitate to demolish a short stretch of old town wall on the way. In Grainger's time, Grainger Street terminated at Bigg Market and it was not until 1862, one year after his death, that Lower Grainger Street was begun and Richard Grainger's dream of linking his central developments with Newcastle's new Central Station started to become a reality. Grainger had argued as early as 1836 that all the private railway companies should share a single central station, rather than having the multiplicity of stations that has since proved to be so problematic in other UK towns and cities.

Newcastle's huge railway station and train shed (1847–51) were designed by none other than John Dobson, one of the most prolific and original Victorian architects, and it is now regarded architecturally as one of the best stations in the country (Fig 22). Other distinctive buildings in Westgate include John Green's Literary and Philosophical Society building (1822); St Mary's Roman Catholic Cathedral by A W N Pugin (1844); House Carpenters Hall (1805–12); William Newton's superb Assembly Rooms (1755); 55–7 Westgate Road (c 1750); and 53 Westgate Road (late 17th or early 18th century) (Fig 23).

Fig 22 *(above) Central Station. Dobson's great curved shed is one of the masterpieces of railway architecture.* [DP000122]

Fig 23 *(right) These fine houses on Westgate Road are a reminder that this was one of the grandest residential streets in Newcastle in the 18th century.* [AA040539]

Part 2
The renaissance of Grainger Town

Grainger Street was still Newcastle's premier shopping street in the years immediately following the Second World War, but soon thereafter Northumberland Street took over this role. From the 1950s onwards the area became increasingly run-down, with high vacancy rates and all the attendant signs of dereliction and decay. By the 1990s the area stood on the brink of a precipice. Unless dramatic action were taken, one of England's grandest urban set pieces would be lost. This chapter charts the remarkable story of Grainger Town's renaissance and identifies the keys that unlocked its potential.

A civic vision for Grainger Town: challenges and solutions

Grainger Town covers approximately 90 acres (36 hectares) and contains over 600 buildings. It comprises a complex mix of buildings and spaces for office, retail, residential, leisure and cultural uses. As we have seen, it possesses a richness of architectural character that makes it of international importance. Virtually all of it is included within Newcastle's Central Conservation Area, which was one of the first to be designated in England. In addition, 244 of its 640 buildings (40%) are listed as being of special architectural or historic interest and of these 12% are listed grade I and 20% grade II★.

The Grainger Town Project, which ran between April 1997 and March 2003, was an ambitious £120-million heritage regeneration programme designed to draw the area back from the precipice of terminal decline and re-establish it as the heart of the city. It was led by the Grainger Town Partnership and supported by English Partnerships (funding subsequently managed by One NorthEast), English Heritage, Newcastle City Council and Tyneside TEC (now the Learning and Skills Council). The project had its origins in 1992 when the Grainger Town Study identified that Grainger Town was exhibiting all the symptoms of urban decay and economic and social decline. It soon became apparent that this could only be dealt with comprehensively and with a clear civic vision.

The causes of decline were varied, complex and often very long term; some were a direct legacy of Grainger's own business practices. Although he died heavily indebted in 1861, his solicitors managed to keep the estate intact until 1901, but at this point it was divided up among many owners in order to make an equitable division. This fragmentation had one unintended benefit, in that it made it difficult later on to assemble property in the hands of a single owner thus discouraging wholesale redevelopment. But the negative effects were only too easy to see by the 1990s: mixed patterns of maintenance and care meant that architectural set pieces such as the terraces ended up as a hotch potch, undermining the impact of the grand design (Fig 24). Other trends, such as the flight of residents from the city centre to the suburbs, often seen as a post-Second World War phenomenon, in fact began in the late 19th century. This brought in its train a diversification of uses but also increasing vacancy levels, particularly on the upper floors.

These trends were exacerbated by a number of factors. In the 1970s, the development of the Eldon Square shopping mall (and then the opening of the Metro underground railway) shifted the focus of retail activity to the northern part of the city centre. In the 1980s and 1990s many businesses moved out, particularly to new developments on the Quayside and Newcastle Business Park or to suburban locations, leaving empty office space behind. Old office space in Grainger Town, even on prestigious Grey Street, was regarded as inflexible and obsolete and refurbishment was seen as too costly. Some developers took advantage of relatively low rentals and used Grainger Town properties as makeweights in their northern property portfolios. Over time this had the effect of inflating values, with investors banking on there being opportunities to redevelop at some time in the future. But developers remained unconvinced as to the long-term profitability of refurbishing the historic buildings themselves. Turning investor confidence around was one of the biggest challenges facing the Grainger Town Project.

Total employment in Newcastle city centre fell by a third in the 1990s from 14,682 in 1992 to 9,892 in 1997. By the mid-1990s the residential population had fallen to 1,200 and was continuing to decline.

Fig 24 *Clayton Street in the mid-1990s: neglect and disuse threatened the future of the area.* *[Grainger Town Partnership]*

These problems were compounded by the low level of car parking provision and the City Council's policy that there should be a car parking space for every new flat. Furthermore, the wide congested streets created barriers to pedestrian movement. By the mid-1990s vacant buildings with a total of over one million square feet of unused floorspace told a story of failure, and there was a serious risk that a vicious circle of low confidence, decline and in some cases dereliction would set in: 47% of the listed buildings were classified as being 'at risk' and a further 29% classified as 'vulnerable' (Fig 25). In addition, the poor quality of the public spaces conveyed a sense of neglect.

Following the 1992 study, conservation-led initiatives such as the 1994 Grainger Town Conservation Area Partnership Scheme tackled the worst buildings at risk and started to halt the spiral of decline using the area's rich architectural assets. By 1996, however, all parties agreed that the environmental, economic, social and cultural issues in the area could not be addressed on an individual basis, building by building. It was clear that sustainable heritage-led regeneration of the whole area was required, but that this would only succeed if physical regeneration was linked to an effective strategy of long-term economic development.

In 1996 English Partnerships, Newcastle City Council and English Heritage appointed consultants EDAW to draw up a comprehensive ten-year strategy for regeneration. This recognised that the revival of Grainger Town as a safe and attractive location to visit, work and live in had to be tackled in a holistic way that respected the area's fine grain and exceptional architecture. EDAW's report set out a civic vision for the area:

> *Grainger Town will become a dynamic and competitive location in the heart of the city. Grainger Town will develop its role in the regional economy within a high quality environment appropriate to a major European Regional Capital. Its reputation for excellence will be focused on leisure, culture, the arts and entrepreneurial activity. Grainger Town will become a distinctive place, a safe and attractive location to work, live and visit.*

Fig 25 *This prominent site at the corner of Grey Street and Mosley Street sent out a signal of failure; now the site has been restored and provides a fitting entrance to Grey Street (see Fig 36). [Grainger Town Partnership]*

This civic vision provided the basis for a six-year (1997–2003), £120-million regeneration programme. The costs were met by both the public and private sectors: £40 million came from English Partnerships, English Heritage, Newcastle City Council and Tyneside TEC, and the balance was raised from the private sector.

This investment aimed to strengthen and develop Grainger Town as a mixed-use historic urban quarter based on seven interrelated regeneration objectives. These provided a multi-layered conservation-planning approach designed to complement the architectural and historic character and significance of the area. The objectives were:

- to develop existing businesses and promote the formation of new businesses
- to secure the reuse of historic buildings and the redevelopment of key sites for office, retail, arts and leisure uses
- to improve training and employment in Grainger Town for residents in the adjoining inner-city wards
- to increase the residential population by creating a range of affordable housing for rent and sale
- to improve the quality of public spaces and traffic management and create an attractive environment which promotes confidence in the area
- to promote Grainger Town as a centre for arts, culture and tourism
- to improve the overall management and marketing of the area.

Six development principles were also established to guide investment within the city centre. These were:

- to extend the retail core south from Eldon Square and Northumberland Street
- to re-introduce housing in the west of the area, focusing on sites on Clayton Street and Grainger Street
- to strengthen the office core around Grey Street, Collingwood Street and Mosley Street
- to create a leisure/cultural corridor to run from St Nicholas's Cathedral through Newgate Street to Stowell Street and from the proposed Centre for Life to Newcastle Opera House

Fig 26 *The Grainger Town Partnership: the staff in 2003. [Grainger Town Partnership]*

- to promote the major public transport nodes and high-profile leisure and tourist attractions to act as magnets in Grainger Town to increase pedestrian flows and footfall throughout the area
- to improve the hard and soft spaces between the buildings to form the glue which binds the various development projects and visitor attractions together.

The Grainger Town Partnership

The regeneration programme was delivered by the Grainger Town Partnership, a company limited by guarantee. Its board brought together a wide range of expertise and had 20 directors, comprising six city councillors, six nominated by the various public agencies involved in the regeneration programme, six from the private sector and two Grainger Town residents. The board was supported by six specialist advisory panels, for example the urban design and public arts panels, and community involvement was built up through monthly meetings of both residents' and business forums. The project was implemented by a dedicated professional delivery team of 14 officers led by project director Chris Oldershaw, based in Central Exchange Buildings at the heart of Grainger Town (Fig 26).

By the end of March 2003 approximately £174 million had been attracted into the Grainger Town area including £146 million from the private sector, comfortably exceeding the project's original lifetime target of £74 million.

During the lifetime of the project the partnership board approved over 70 schemes with a grant requirement of over £35 million. Notable achievements included:

- 1,506 jobs created directly by the project and a further 800 jobs created in Grainger Town generally, encouraged by increased confidence in the area
- over 286 new businesses set up, largely through the Grainger Town Business Development Fund and Project North East's Youth Enterprise Support Scheme

Figs 27a and b *Before and after: Market Street was transformed in 1999 by refurbishment, occupation by new shops and new uses for the upper floors. [Grainger Town Partnership]*

- the provision of over 80,900 square metres of new or refurbished commercial floorspace
- over 289 flats and apartments completed with a further 283 in the process of completion, many within an area (Grainger Street and Clayton Street) with a high concentration of 'buildings at risk'
- 121 buildings (many of them listed and classified as 'buildings at risk') brought back into use (Figs 27a and b)
- major improvements to public spaces completed throughout the area based on an urban design framework provided by Gillespies, a Glasgow-based consultancy
- Grey's Monument successfully repaired and cleaned with the help of the Heritage Lottery Fund (Fig 28)
- Westgate House, an intrusive 11-storey 1960s office block on Westgate Road, acquired by One NorthEast for demolition and mixed-use redevelopment (Fig 29)
- Wards Building on High Bridge acquired for extension to the Waygood Gallery and conversion of former warehouses for artists' studios and workshops
- major Conservation Area Partnership/Heritage Economic Regeneration schemes completed, jointly funded by English Heritage and Newcastle City Council.

In addition to physical improvements the partnership supported and organised numerous successful business, arts and cultural events, including an international heritage conference that focused on the regeneration of Europe's historic cities (Figs 30a–d). The conference marked the launch of INHERIT, a network of historic cities dedicated to the promotion and exchange of best practice in heritage-led regeneration.

Fig 28 *(above) The statue of Earl Grey, badly scarred by 150 years of pollution, was restored in 2000. [Grainger Town Partnership]*

Fig 29 *(above right) How damage can be reversed. The towering slab of Westgate House, 'unspeakably ugly and intrusive' (Grundy et al 1992, 491): its demolition to restore the scale of the urban landscape was a flagship project of the Grainger Town Partnership. [AA040518]*

The success of the project has generated significant and positive change in Grainger Town. Overall this has meant that:

■ the long-term future of the area's architectural heritage is now secure
■ the physical, economic and demographic decline of Grainger Town has been reversed
■ there is renewed confidence in the retail, commercial and leisure markets in the area
■ the area has had its character and quality restored and has a new-found vitality.

Three particularly significant problems faced the partnership. One, as we have seen, was the lack of investor confidence in the area's future. This was overcome by the distribution of informative and promotional material, by active marketing and by vigorous local and regional promotion. The successful development of a number of demonstration

Figs 30a–d *Spreading the word: the Grainger Town Project involved the publication of a number of education packs aimed at school children; public arts and street theatre; a special fashion show in the Assembly Rooms; and a major international conference. [All photographs Grainger Town Partnership]*

Regenerating Europe's Historic Cities
3 - 5 July 2002, Newcastle upon Tyne, UK

An International Conference hosted
by the Grainger Town Partnership

 Investing in **Heritage**

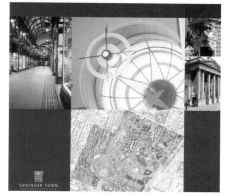

projects and flagship schemes also showed the area's potential. The second problem related to the practical issues involved in the refurbishment and reuse of historic buildings: for example, the high level of multi-occupation and the fragmented ownership of many of the Georgian terraces made access for surveys difficult. The third major problem – entirely unanticipated when the project began – was the loss in 1999 of Partnership Investment Programme funding from English Partnerships, due to EC decisions on infringements to State Aid rules and the subsequent reduced funding allocations from One NorthEast. All three issues presented severe difficulties for the project, and their impact had to be handled extremely carefully in order to protect investment confidence and maintain the programme's momentum.

Best practice in heritage-led regeneration

The Grainger Town Project is now widely recognised as an exemplary regeneration scheme and its approach is being applied both in the UK and abroad. An independent interim evaluation concluded that the project had been successful in 'promoting change, reversing decline and helping to produce more positive perceptions of the area. The project has been well managed and the process of regeneration has proved effective and worked well' (Robinson *et al* 2001, 60). In 2001 it received a British Urban Regeneration Association Best Practice award. The judges commented that the transformation of the area – something that would not have seemed possible a few years ago – showed how effective partnership between the public sector, local businesses and the local community could achieve rapid improvements and had contributed greatly to the project's success. More recently the project has received a commendation from the Royal Town Planning Institute and Grey Street was voted 'Best Loved Street in Britain' by the Commission for Architecture and the Built Environment (CABE) and BBC Radio 4 listeners. So what key lessons have been learnt?

- The need for a heritage audit and detailed survey of the area at the start of a regeneration programme to establish the significance of its historic environment and the main issues that need to be addressed.
- The need to change perceptions of heritage by promoting a new 'civic vision' with a strong emphasis on a high quality environment, city living and culture.
- The importance of 'early wins' and the selective use of compulsory purchase order powers to demonstrate resolve and commitment. All regeneration projects need high profile early successes to send a strong message to the property market that positive change is underway.
- The importance of creating an ethos of quality and excellence in design through demonstration projects, informative and promotional handbooks, design guides and location marketing.
- The importance of a coherent yet flexible strategy to help build up investment confidence based on a detailed assessment of the area's strengths and weaknesses.
- The need to raise aspirations in the wider community about what can be achieved by learning from best practice in the UK and other European cities.
- The importance of integration with an emphasis on a holistic conservation-planning approach to regeneration.
- The need to establish broad-based partnerships to provide leaders for change and community involvement.
- The importance of having a dedicated professional project team, based in the area and with strong links to the development industry.

The future of Grainger Town

During the last two years of the project the partnership developed a forward strategy, in line with Newcastle City Council policies and the Council's Unitary Development Plan, to ensure that the process of

regeneration continued after the termination of the partnership on
31 March 2003 and to provide a seamless transition to successor bodies.
The forward strategy comprises five key elements:

- a critical and objective assessment of the project's achievements in
  relation to the original vision
- proposals for future action to enhance the city centre's overall
  attractiveness and viability after the project
- successor arrangements for the partnership board, forums and panels
- an assessment of the financial implications of the forward strategy for
  such bodies as the City Council
- arrangements for protecting the assets created by the partnership, for
  example through agreed management and maintenance contracts
  and service level agreements for improvements to public spaces and
  other key projects.

In addition to the forward strategy, the Grainger Town Partnership
also established a maintenance charter that set out the maintenance
requirements of the area up to 2008. This included elements such as the
cleaning and repair of the high quality public areas, the innovative
public art and the bespoke Grainger Town street furniture.

The strategy and charter will be monitored by the City Council's
city centre team and panel who will champion future improvements and
help to protect and maintain the Grainger Town legacy. Both One
NorthEast and the city centre panel will receive regular reports on
progress in maintaining and managing the project's legacy.

The project's impact on all facets of Grainger Town life is now clear
for all to see and its successes are increasingly being recognised both at
home and abroad. The work of the project has generated an
environmental, economic, social and cultural renaissance that has
enhanced the quality and reinforced the identity of the city centre,
bringing life back to the heart of Newcastle. The area has clearly turned
the corner and its future as an internationally significant historic urban
quarter and a European regional capital now seems secure.

Part 3:
A walking tour of Grainger Town

Introduction

This tour is intended as a guide to the principal buildings of Grainger Town, which are marked on the map at the back of this booklet and numbered in bold in the text. A suggested route around the main sites is given below, but you may choose your own and so a trail has not been marked on the map. The full tour should take 2–3 hours to complete.

Many of the buildings and spaces described in the tour have undergone repair and refurbishment and/or have been turned to new uses, and the Grainger Town Partnership (GTP) has been a key agent in assisting these changes as part of its policy of regeneration.

Many individual buildings have reaped the benefits of GTP involvement. The redevelopment of Nos 2–8 Grey Street was a GTP flagship scheme, as has been the replacement of Westgate House and Norwich Union House with buildings more appropriate to this historic area; a demonstration that bold regeneration can include the removal of some of the least successful of our modern developments. The former Central Post Office, having lain vacant for a number of years in the 1990s, was bought in 1998–9 and refurbished to provide mixed use with a GTP grant. On a smaller scale, though no less interesting, the 18th-century house at No. 7 Rosemary Lane was restored with grant assistance from the GTP Heritage Economic Regeneration Scheme.

Continuing Richard Grainger's tradition of combining residential with commercial space, a GTP grant helped convert Victoria Buildings on Grainger Street, originally built as offices over shops, to provide apartments on the upper floors. A number of Living Over The Shop schemes by Housing Associations such as Home, assisted by GTP, have transformed Clayton Street by restoring and bringing back into use a number of important listed buildings once classified as 'buildings at risk'. In addition, the GTP Shopfront Improvement Grant Scheme has refurbished a number of commercial properties, by replacing inappropriate later shopfronts or restoring early survivals to their historical integrity.

Another prominent example of GTP's achievements is Grey's Monument and statue, which was restored in 2000. Artist Simon Watkinson was commissioned to design a setting for the monument as part of GTP's public arts programme, and the creative lighting provides a dramatic set piece at night at this focal point of the city. The area around the monument was part of the first phase of GTP's 'public realm strategy', which is in evidence across Grainger Town. The performance space outside the Theatre Royal, for example, incorporates a millennium time capsule, buried by schoolchildren in May 2000 and marked by an X in the paving. On the other side of Grainger Town, Cardinal Hume's statue and the memorial garden in which it stands were part-funded by GTP as part of this strategy.

Assistance from the Grainger Town Partnership has ensured the future of this rich mix of buildings, spaces and uses, which creates the vibrancy and wealth of character that confirms Grainger Town as a historic city centre of national significance.

The tour

The tour starts at Grey's Monument at the head of Grey Street, which can be easily reached from Monument Metro station. Car parks are marked on the map.

Grey's Monument (1) (Fig 31) (1838, listed grade I) was erected to commemorate Earl Grey and his contribution to the passing of the Great Reform Bill in 1832. Designed by Benjamin Green, the monument has a Roman Doric column of hard millstone grit 135-feet tall, set on a base of local sandstone. It is topped with a limestone statue of Charles Earl Grey by the sculptor Edward Hodges Baily.

Fig 31 *High quality public area works and lighting display the grandeur of the setting and give an extra dimension to Newcastle's lively nightlife. [AA040881]*

Fig 32 *The great sweep of Grey Street from the north. [AA040534]*

Walk in a southerly direction down Grey Street, described by Pevsner as 'one of the best streets in England' (Grundy *et al* 1992, 487) (Fig 32). John Dobson designed the south-eastern section, and John Wardle and George Walker are thought to have designed the rest, all for Richard Grainger. The street followed the line of the Lort Burn and required the demolition of the old Theatre Royal and the old butcher market. The majority of the buildings on the street are listed grade I or II★. Grey Street is, perhaps, the best exponent of 'Tyneside Classical', with a sequence of large palace-fronted terraces made up of plain sections alternating with pilastered pavilions and wings. In 2002 it was voted 'Britain's Best Loved Street' by CABE and listeners of BBC Radio 4.

At 102 Grey Street you will find Lloyds Bank **(2)** (*c* 1839, listed grade II★). The architect of the building is not known. Originally providing a bank on the ground floor and housing on the upper floors, the building's interior was extensively remodelled in 1987.

In Grey Street and elsewhere around Grainger Town you will see bespoke street furniture. Designed by Insite Environments and with artwork by Cate Watkinson and Julia Darling, the furniture was installed by the Grainger Town Partnership as part of its Public Arts Programme (Fig 33).

About halfway down Grey Street is the Theatre Royal **(3)** (1836–7, listed grade I), designed by John and Benjamin Green for Richard Grainger when David Stephenson's 1788 theatre was demolished to make way for Grey Street (*see* cover picture). Grainger was committed to providing a replacement and its location on Grey Street ensured that it had maximum effect on the townscape. Imposing externally, the theatre was planned around a three-storey entrance rotunda with a finely decorated dome: off the rotunda opened lobbies, staircases and the first tier of large and small stage boxes. A fire gutted the theatre in 1899 and a new interior was designed by architect Frank Matcham in 1901. This Edwardian interior was remodelled again in 1987 by Renton Howard Wood Levin Partnership, but Matcham's balconies and boxes were retained (Fig 34).

Fig 33 *'Nine things to do on a bench: wait and see':*
part of the public space improvements in Grey Street.
[AA040880]

Farther down the street you will see Nos 52–78 Grey Street, Lloyds
Court **(4)** (*c* 1836, listed grade II★), designed by John Dobson for Richard
Grainger (*see* Fig 13). Dobson's east side of Grey Street is more reserved
and less ornamented than Wardle's west side. Numbers 52–78 include a
small corner pavilion and a large seven-window-wide pavilion section that
was originally four houses. In 1996 Newcastle City Council approved a
scheme by Terry Farrell Architects in which Nos 52–60 were restored and
extended to the rear and the façade of Nos 62–78 was retained to provide
a frontage to a new open-plan office space. While the principle of
façadism is generally not permissible under Council policy or condoned

Fig 34 *The interior of the Theatre Royal. [AA040511]*

by English Heritage, it was concluded that the scheme ensured the successful long-term use of the property and retained the rhythm and harmony of this section of the townscape along Grey Street.

Farther along on the west side of Grey Street are Nos 33–9 Grey Street **(5)** (*c* 1835, listed grade II⋆), built to house a branch of the Bank of England (*see* Fig 16). Probably designed by John Wardle for Richard Grainger, this is the centrepiece of the western side of Grey Street and its palatial elevation emphasises its pivotal position.

Retrace your steps and turn east along High Bridge and then right into Pilgrim Street (possibly the oldest route in Newcastle). At No. 98 Pilgrim Street is Alderman Fenwick's House **(6)** (listed grade I), which dates from

Fig 35 *Alderman Fenwick's House, Pilgrim Street: the finest 17th-century brick house remaining in central Newcastle. [AA040540]*

the late 17th century with 18th-century alterations (Fig 35). Probably one of the grandest mansions of its time, it indicates that Pilgrim Street was a place of residence for the wealthy merchants of Newcastle in the 17th century. The house was used as a coaching inn from 1780 and as Newcastle's Liberal Club from 1884. Empty for over 25 years and in a derelict state, it was taken over in 1982 by the Tyne and Wear Building Preservation Trust which began a sensitive restoration scheme, finally completed in 1998.

Carry on down Pilgrim Street and turn right into Mosley Street. On the corner of Mosley Street and Grey Street are the prominent Nos 2–12 Grey Street **(7)** (1842, listed grade II). With its neighbours Nos 14–16, built in phases between 1879 (No. 16) and 1908 (No. 10, the last part of Grey Street to be completed), the building lay vacant for nearly 20 years.

Under the threat of compulsory purchase, the owners entered into a legal agreement with Newcastle City Council to refurbish the buildings. Under the terms of the agreement, the freehold of the site was transferred to the City Council and the developers were given a license to undertake conversion to an agreed programme and standard. Upon successful completion the freehold transfers back to the owner (Fig 36 *see also* Fig 25).

Cross Grey Street and continue along Mosley Street then turn right into Cloth Market. You are now in the medieval market area of Newcastle, renowned as one of the main party areas of the city at night (*see* Figs 17 and 18).

Fig 36 *The corner of Mosley Street and Grey Street. Formerly vacant buildings at risk are being refurbished as a hotel. [AA040914]*

Fig 37 *The long narrow yard of the Old George recalls the medieval origins of the plots around the market place. A ramp once gave access to first-floor stables. [DP000100]*

At Nos 6–8 Cloth Market is Balmbra's public house **(8)** (1902, listed grade II) by A Stockwell. Named after John Balmbra, landlord of the previous premises in the mid-19th century when the pub was called the Wheat Sheaf Inn, this building is the most celebrated public house on Tyneside; in its concert room in 1862 George Ridley, a popular local singer and composer, first sang his song 'Blaydon Races' in which the pub is mentioned.

Farther up from Balmbra's you will see a small alleyway called White Hart Yard, which is a medieval burgage lane. It is the widest of all the Cloth Market burgage lanes, most of which are only 3 feet wide. White Hart Yard takes its name from an ancient coaching inn. The buildings retain fragments of 17th century and possibly even earlier work, but are mainly of later date. The central roadway of cobbles and wheel-worn granite gutters and the overhead lifting gantries on the south side are a reminder of the yard's earlier industrial uses.

Carry on north-west up Cloth Market and you will find Old George Yard and the Old George Public House **(9)** (listed grade II). Parts of the building date from the early 17th century, but a succession of later occupiers made alterations to suit their changing needs. The cobbled yard (Fig 37) has a great deal of historical character and charm, and one feature of particular interest are the two-storey stables on the north side: a ramp formerly gave access for horses to reach the upper floor.

As you enter Bigg Market you will see the Half Moon Inn and Chambers **(10)** (1902–5, listed grade II) by Simpson, Lawson and Rayne for Arrols of Alloa (brewers). The present highly decorated building replaced an earlier Half Moon Inn on the same site and is clearly designed to make a bold architectural statement. Note the half-moon motifs in the decorative ironwork of the balconies.

At the far end of Bigg Market is the J H Rutherford memorial **(11)** (1894, listed grade II) by Charles E Errington. Rutherford was a doctor, preacher, educationalist and friend to the poor. Originally outside the Cathedral of St Nicholas, the memorial was moved to Bigg Market in 1903.

Now turn back along the south-west side of the market and along Groat Market to the junction with Collingwood Street. Opposite you will see St Nicholas's Cathedral **(12)** (listed grade I), dating mainly from the mid-14th century (Fig 38). This former parish church with its beautiful spire became a cathedral in 1882 when Newcastle was formally made a city. The tower crown was rebuilt twice, in 1608 and in the 19th century, and repaired in the 18th century and in 1994. Inside the building, the 15th-century Roger Thornton Brass, the 17th-century Maddison family monument and the marble memorial bust of Admiral Lord Collingwood are all of interest.

On the western side of St Nicholas Street is the former Central Post Office (now Red Box Buildings) **(13)**, constructed in 1871–4 to designs by James Williams and refurbished by Alan J Smith of Red Box Design. Its imposing classical elevation combines a huge two-storey recessed entrance porch with four full storeys around it (Fig 39). Note the giant block lettering in the frieze showing the building's original use.

Walk back onto Collingwood Street and carry on south-westwards then turn left into Westgate Road. On the southern side of the street you will find three buildings that are of particular interest – Bolbec Hall, the Literary and Philosophical Society Building, and Neville Hall and Wood Memorial Hall (Fig 40). The first building in the group is Bolbec Hall **(14)** (1907, listed grade II), which was designed by Frank Rich in a Free Italian style, in sharp contrast to its neighbour. The building was built as offices to provide a rental income for the Literary and Philosophical Society. The central building in the group is the earliest: John Green's Literary and Philosophical Society Building **(15)** (1822, listed grade II★) was built for the Society (founded in 1793) in the Greek Revival style fashionable with local architects at the time, and John Green rivalled John Dobson with the quality of his work. To the right of the 'Lit and Phil' stands Neville Hall and Wood Memorial Hall **(16)** (1870, listed grade II). This Gothic structure was designed by A M Dunn and a lecture theatre was added by Cackett and Burns Dick in 1902 (Fig 41).

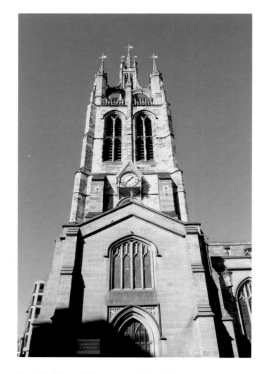

Fig 38 *(above) The tower of St Nicholas's Cathedral topped by a crown and miniature spire; a distinctive feature of the Newcastle skyline. [DP00099]*

Fig 39 *(right) The former Central Post Office, built 1871–4 and now refurbished for offices and residential use. [AA040524]*

Fig 40 *(below left) The grouping of Bolbec Hall (left), the Literary and Philosophical Society's headquarters (centre) and Neville Hall and Wood Memorial Hall (right) is an essay in changing style, from the classical to the Gothic to Edwardian Baroque. [AA040536]*

Fig 41 *(below right) The lecture theatre attached to Neville Hall, used by the North of England Institute of Mining and Mechanical Engineers. [AA040515]*

It is occupied by the North of England Institute of Mining and Mechanical Engineers, which played an essential role in the successful development of industry in the region.

Return to Collingwood Street, the north side of which shows further contrasts of style. Collingwood Buildings, Nos 28–62 **(17)** (1899, listed grade II), on the corner of Collingwood Street and Pudding Chare,

Fig 42 *28–62 Collingwood Street, built in 1899 as a hotel, offices and shops and adapted in 1903 to include a bank. [AA040519]*

was designed as a hotel, offices and shops by Oliver and Leeson but adapted by Cackett and Burns Dick in 1903 to include a bank (Fig 42). It was built in the Free Baroque style popular at the time. Currently in use as a bar, the 1903 banking hall is impressive and has rich marble walls, mahogany panelling and fittings and a high-quality decorative plasterwork ceiling.

Across Pudding Chare is the site of Westgate House and Norwich Union House **(18)** (1965–71, by Cartwright Woolatt and Partners) (*see* Fig 29). For decades an intrusive landmark straddling Westgate Road, they were a constant reminder of Newcastle's aspiration to be the 'Brasilia of the North' during the 1960s. Next door, in contrast, the Union Rooms **(19)** (1877, listed grade II) by M P Manning, were built as a club in an elaborate French Renaissance style.

Turn right and walk along Rosemary Lane to No. 7 **(20)** (listed grade II), an interesting small brick and pantile house with shaped gables dating from the 18th century (Fig 43). It is the only survivor of a varied row of 18th-century houses that used to overlook a small open green to the north-west of St John's Church.

Walk along the cobbled St John Street to its junction with Grainger Street. The southern section of Grainger Street, south of Bigg Market, was originally a narrower street called St John's Lane, which was widened in 1869 to provide better access for vehicles to the Central Station. In less than five years it had been developed with massive Victorian commercial structures. No. 30 Grainger Street **(21)** (1884–7, listed grade II) was designed by John Johnson as offices for the Newcastle and Gateshead Gas Company. The last property to be developed in the street, it has a metal-framed structure clad in an authentic French chateau fashion.

Farther up Grainger Street are Nos 42–50, Victoria Buildings **(22)** (1874, listed grade II), designed by Matthew Thompson in an elaborate Italianate style.

Fig 43 *Surrounded by later buildings, the 18th century house at No. 7 Rosemary Lane has ornamental Dutch gables. [AA040525]*

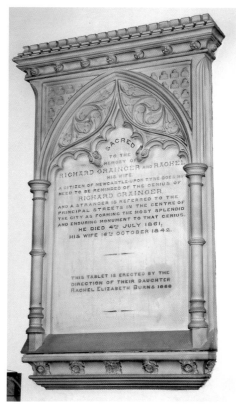

Now turn south along Grainger Street to the junction with Westgate Road. On your left is the Church of St John the Baptist **(23)** (listed grade I) which dates mostly from the 14th and 15th centuries. One of Newcastle's four medieval churches, it is a neat parish church with a three-storey tower crowned with corner finials (Fig 44a). This was Richard Grainger's own parish church when he lived on Clayton Street West and his life and work are commemorated in a plaque inside the church (Fig 44b).

Cross Westgate Road and continue south down Grainger Street, then turn right into Neville Street. To your left you will see Newcastle Central Station **(24)** (listed grade I). The main building of 1847–51 was designed by John Dobson, and the immense portico was added in 1863 by Thomas Prosser, extended *c* 1890 by W Bell. The imposing station, with its huge curving shed and impressive iron roof, is architecturally one of the best in the country and a fitting gate of entry to a regional capital (*see* Fig 22).

Fig 44a *(above left) The Church of St John the Baptist, one of Newcastle's four medieval churches.* [AA040517]

Fig 44b *(above) The memorial plaque to Richard Grainger inside his parish church of St John the Baptist.* [DP00095]

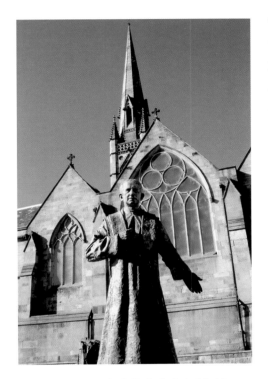

Fig 45 *The Roman Catholic Cathedral of St Mary, by A W N Pugin, forms the backdrop to Nigel Boonham's statue of Cardinal Hume. [DP00086]*

Turn right into Bewick Street. To your left is a statue of Cardinal Hume, one of the North East's most famous sons **(25)**. The statue stands in a memorial garden representing the Northumbrian island of Lindisfarne; both were designed by sculptor Nigel Boonham and the statue was unveiled by Queen Elizabeth II on her Golden Jubilee tour (Fig 45). Ahead of you is St Mary's Roman Catholic Cathedral **(26)** (listed grade I). The complex is the product of six different architects over a space of 140 years, with the body of the church by A W N Pugin (1842–4) and the tower and spire by A M Dunn and E J Hansom (*c* 1872). Grouped around the church are the baptistry chapel, the cathedral library and the presbytery. There is some good stained glass to be seen around the complex.

Travel along Bewick Street, turn left into Clayton Street West, then right into Forth Place and walk along to the junction with Waterloo Street. To your left you will see the Richard Grainger Memorial Fountain **(27)** (1892, listed grade II) by Elswick Court Marble Works Company, Newcastle. Originally located farther up Waterloo Street, the fountain was moved to its present position in 1981 as part of the Clayton Street West housing scheme (*see* Fig 15a).

Travel north along Waterloo Street then turn left to Westgate Road. Westgate Road is a very ancient route, part of the cross-Pennine road between Carlisle and Newcastle. It was important enough to merit a gateway in the town wall when it was built in the 13th century and became a prime residential quarter within the walled area in the 18th century.

On the south side of the street you will see the Newcastle Opera House **(28)** (1867, listed grade I), by W B Parnell for the local entrepreneur Joseph Cowen (Fig 46a). Originally known as the Tyne Theatre and Opera House, it was built as a rival to the Theatre Royal. Although Parnell had little experience of theatre design he created one of the most architecturally significant buildings of the type, with a simple, elegant auditorium (Fig 46b) and a backstage area full of ingenious gadgetry.

Fig 46a *The Newcastle Opera House, Westgate Road, with a newly created public open space on Bath Lane in the foreground. [AA040919]*

Fig 46b *The interior of the Opera House retains the original auditorium, with its triple tier of balconies. [AA040514]*

Fig 47 *A detail of the sumptuous 18th-century plasterwork which adorns the interior of Nos 55–7 Westgate Road. [DP00079]*

In 1985 a fire destroyed much of the stage area and the understage machinery, but careful restoration between 1985 and 1987 returned everything to full working order.

Walk east along Westgate Road towards the junction with Grainger Street and you will see two important buildings **(29)** (*see* Fig 23). No. 53 Westgate Road (listed grade II) dates from the late 17th or early 18th century. Brick with fine ashlar details, it was built as a substantial town house reportedly for Lady Clavering but is now offices, some of which retain original decorative plasterwork. Nos 55–7 Westgate Road (listed grade II★) dates from *c* 1750. The fine ashlar elevation, with giant pilasters and heavy eaves cornice, reveals the house as an important residence, and this is borne out internally where fine 18th-century plasterwork survives in the ground and first-floor rooms (Fig 47).

Retrace your steps and turn right into Fenkle Street. The elegance and quality of Westgate Road in the 18th century is seen again here in the

Assembly Rooms **(30)** (1774–6, listed grade II★) by William Newton, set back a little way from the road on your right (see Fig 4). The social centre for town and country, the Assembly Rooms were designed in classical style, with a high pedimented central section and lower flanking wings. Decoration is concentrated in the central area, where giant Ionic columns rise from the rusticated ground floor to support the pediment. On the first floor the lower wings have arched recesses with plain windows. Only the later canopy across the entrance mars the elegance of the main front. The interior, which includes a ballroom, cardrooms, newsroom and a huge supper room, is a superb example of decorative design (Fig 48). It has played host to distinguished visitors such as Charles Dickens, The Duke of Wellington, Edward VII and George V.

Opposite the Assembly Rooms stands the imposing Cross House **(31)**. The first Cross House was a 17th-century brick mansion, once the home of Ralph Carr, founder of Newcastle's first bank in 1755. This was replaced by the present building in 1911. The architects Cackett and Burns Dick used an innovative reinforced-concrete structural system

Fig 48 *(above) The huge supper room of the Assembly Rooms: over 450 people could be accommodated on grand social occasions. [AA040513]*

Fig 49 *(left) Clayton Street at night: once more a place to live. [AA040888]*

Fig 50 *Charlotte Square, built in the late 18th century. The houses around the square had shared private use of the central garden. [AA040521]*

patented by the Hennebique Company and developed on Tyneside. The ferro-concrete frame was clad in fashionable Portland stone.

Travel along Fenkle Street to the junction with Clayton Street. Clayton Street dates from 1837 and was probably built to designs by Walker and Wardle for Richard Grainger (Fig 49). It was named after John Clayton, town clerk and Grainger's great friend and supporter. It is inferior in design and materials to Grainger Street and much inferior to Grey Street.

Cross over Clayton Street and continue on to Charlotte Square **(32)**. Designed by William Newton in 1770, this is Newcastle's earliest London-style square and was named after Queen Charlotte, wife of George III (Fig 50). It was speculatively built with substantial brick houses on three sides around a garden reserved for the exclusive use of the occupiers of the square.

Fig 51 *The splendidly restored meeting room of one of the craft guilds in Blackfriars. [AA040538]*

Turn right then left along Monk Street to the Blackfriars complex **(33)** (listed grade I). This was built by Dominican friars and dates from the late 13th and early 14th centuries (*see* Fig 19). The Dominican order of friars, founded in 1216, had established a Newcastle house by 1239. The friary was arranged in the usual way with a church and, on its south side, ranges of buildings and covered walkways around an open square or cloister. After the dissolution in 1539 the friars were evicted and most of the property was bought by the Newcastle Corporation and leased to nine of the town's craft guilds as a meeting place and to provide almshouses. By the middle of the 20th century only two guilds remained. From the 1950s the City Council (formerly the Corporation), having lost the title to the properties, began to acquire them again and in 1975 began a restoration programme which was completed in 1981 (Fig 51). The complex is now occupied by a restaurant, craft workshops and the North East Civic Trust.

From Blackfriars travel west to Stowell Street. Begun in 1824, this street was built through the Blackfriars precinct, parallel with the town wall.

Fig 52 *Fortress Newcastle: an impression of the walled town can still be gained from this view along Bath Lane. [DP00087]*

It was a dead end until the 1850s when a gap was made through the wall south of Heber Tower to link Stowell Street with Bath Lane. It is now the heart of Newcastle's Chinatown, lined with colourful restaurants and grocery stores (*see* Fig 20).

Turn left to the end of Stowell Street and left again into Bath Lane, where you will see the best preserved and most easily viewed part of Newcastle's medieval wall **(34)** (listed grade I). Dating from the late 13th century, it survives here nearly to its original height of over 20 feet (Fig 52). In the whole circuit of the wall there were six principal gates and other lesser gates and doorways. Of its 17 towers, Durham Tower (within this stretch of wall) is the least altered and best preserved. In spite of the destruction of parts of the wall and of all of the gates in the 18th and 19th centuries, only the medieval walls of York, Chester, Chichester and Southampton survive in a more complete state.

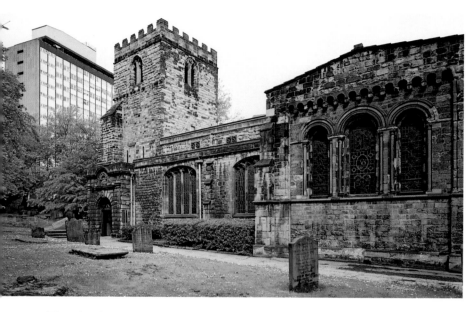

Fig 53 *St Andrew's Church, a hidden gem in the busy centre of Newcastle. The Norman chancel arch is spectacular. [AA040912]*

Turn back and travel north to the end of Stowell Street then turn right and walk along St Andrew's Street to the junction with Newgate Street. St Andrew's Church **(35)** (listed grade I) is on the corner to your left (Fig 53). The building dates mainly from the 12th to 15th centuries and is thought to be both the first church to be established in Newcastle and the possible location of the Anglian settlement that may have occupied the site after the abandonment of the Roman fort and town. The spectacular Norman chancel arch demonstrates that the church was already important in the 12th century.

Across from St Andrew's Church, on Newgate Street, is the North-East Co-operative Stores building **(36)** (1931–2, listed grade II). This is Newcastle's most impressive Art Deco building of the 1930s, and was designed by the Co-operative Wholesale Society architect L G Ekins. Of particular note inside is the steel handrail supported by polished metal figures. This store replaced an earlier Co-op store of 1870 on the same site and was extended at the west end in 1959.

Fig 54 *Murton House, 68–72 Grainger Street. The five-bay end pavilion was probably built as a pair of houses over shops. [AA040529]*

Continue south-east to the end of Newgate Street and turn left into Grainger Street, the second in status of Richard Grainger's planned streets which was probably designed by Walker and Wardle. On the eastern side, on the corner with Bigg Market, is Murton House Nos 68–72 **(37)** (1836, listed grade II). Part of a long terrace, the five-bay end pavilion provides a decorative stop to the street elevation (Fig 54). A number of the shopfronts along Grainger Street, for example Nos 105–9 and Nos 129–31, have been refurbished through Grainger Town

Fig 55 *The elegant simplicity of Grainger's shopfronts has been re-interpreted in the modern restoration funded by the Grainger Town Shopfront Improvement Grant Scheme. [DP00073]*

Partnership's Shopfront Improvement Grant Scheme, to provide a much more coherent street scene (Fig 55).

Farther along Grainger Street on your left is the Grainger Market **(38)** (listed grade I). The building, dating from 1835, was designed by John Dobson and built on the site of the Nuns Field. The banquet held to open the market, presided over by the Mayor, was attended by around 2,000

Fig 56 *The busy interior of Grainger Market, with stalls arranged in long alleys: in the foreground is one of the market's most attractive stalls, which retains the frontage created to house Marks and Spencer's Penny Bazaar. [AA040917]*

men and 300 women, the latter separately accommodated on a specially erected balcony. The market complex forms a complete block, defined by four streets of Grainger's standard three-storey terraces of shops and offices (*see* Fig 14). The market hall occupies the central well formed by these ranges. Lit by clerestorey windows, the hall has five longitudinal and four transverse avenues of shops and 14 entrances. Among the shops is a rare survival of a Marks and Spencer Penny Bazaar (Fig 56). The vegetable market was remodelled after a fire in 1901. Perhaps the best surviving example in the country of a large early covered market, it is undoubtedly of national importance. The market is closed on Sundays.

Continue along Grainger Street towards Grey's Monument. On your right you will see the Central Exchange Buildings (1837, probably by Walker and Wardle for Richard Grainger), incorporating the Central

Arcade **(39)** (1906, by J Oswald and Sons). Both buildings are listed grade II★. Richard Grainger intended the complex to be a corn exchange but it opened in 1837 as a subscription newsroom and within three years had nearly 1,600 members. It later became an art gallery, a concert hall and in 1897 a vaudeville theatre, then was totally gutted by fire in 1901. The whole building was extensively refurbished in 1906 and the present shop-lined Central Arcade, beautifully decorated with excellent faience tiles from Burmantofts, Leeds, was cut through from Grey Street to Market Street with a link to Grainger Street (Fig 57). Parts of the upper floors have been converted into 17 exclusive maisonettes.

In the paving adjacent to the Grainger Street entrance to the Central Arcade is a commemorative plate to Richard Grainger, designed by Charlie Holmes to mark the bicentennary of Grainger's birth. It was the first piece of public art created as part of the Grainger Town Partnership's public arts programme (*see* Fig 15b).

This completes the circuit. You are now back at your starting point, Grey's Monument: the focal point of Richard Grainger's redevelopment.

Fig 57 *The Central Arcade, with original shopfronts on the ground floor and upper-floor offices and flats. [DP00084]*